IN THIS CORNER

Antonio Creti • Salvatore Marafioti

IN THIS CORNER

anecdotes, testimonies and fighting words from annals of the boxing world

GREMESE INTERNATIONAL

Editor:
Lynn Yuill

Jacket design by:
Carlo Soldatini

Phototypeset by:
Videografica '93 - Rome

Photography:
Used with permission from
«Boxe Ring»

Photolithography by:
Bielleci - Rome

Printed by:
Tipografia Atena - Rome

© 1995 Gremese International s.r.l.
P.O.B. 14335 - 00149 Rome

ISBN 88-7301-048-2

Preface

The adventure of two men who without any other weapons except their arms face each other and compete in the ring belongs to the history of Man. From ancient Mesopotamia, to Greece, it has crossed the Roman Empire and overcome the Middle Ages to land in our times with its cargo of contradictions and paradoxes.

Boxing has an innate, indisputable harshness. In the ring there is neither mediation nor compromise. Predictions, agreements, bets, combines: everything happens outside of the fight perimeter, where the two boxers are during the highest point of their solitude, with their fear and courage. One in front of the other waiting for the bell with respect for the rules and fair play.

For this the song of boxing has been sung by the lettered and the artists, and has inspired writers and poets. Because it is not only a sport, not only competition, not only the challenge of the unknown: it is also and above all a measure of two characters who face and confront each other with toughness and energy risking their own safety. Boxing puts at the centre of its essence the duel between two enemies and rivals ready to use all their energy to win. Two bitter opponents who embrace and compliment each other at the end of the match. Often, indeed, the tougher the fight, the warmer the embrace will be, almost to symbolise the common struggle for survival. This is the fascination of boxing; the paradox of an endless duel, mystic and profane, between good and evil, between today and eternity that embodies life, of which like many have said remains a splendid metaphor.

This book is dedicated to boxing. A book of aphorisms and photographs more complex than it would seem. The boxing world, although Norman Mailer thinks differently, is a world of free spirits which are often impulsive and extroverted. It is a world filled with people who speak freely, often suggestively. Many boxers have written autobiographies and screenplays for both stage and cinema and many writers who are fascinated with the ring have produced works drenched with the

*P*aintings on Greek vases show boxers in a traditional pose so close to one another that each one has a foot placed right in front of or behind that of the other. There wasn't much space for the footwork of today that lets boxers move around rapidly, from right to left, or front to back. Moving back, as per the code of honour, was considered a sign of cowardice. Avoiding the punches of the opponent by moving away was considered dishonourable.

Eric Dunning

Red-figured Lynn from the 6th century B.C. The fighter on the left is bleeding profusely.

A vase by the "Painter of Nikosthenes" from the 6th
century B.C. The athlete on the left is bleeding
from the nose.

*Fighters in ancient Greece fought until the bitter end. But if the fight
went on too long a judge could order the two rivals to give or take a
blow to the head without defending himself until one of the two couldn't
continue the fight. In short, It emphasised the culminating moment, the
verdict, as the most important part of the confrontation, it was more
important that the fight itself.*

Eric Dunning

suggestive atmosphere that only boxing can offer. Our work was therefore to give synthesis, interpretation, and an editorial body to the plethora of anecdotes and sentences that have subsisted in the "spoken" world of boxing.

As a tribute to and with respect for this it was thought to maintain unadulterated the casual element that lies at the base of this work. Over the years in fact, methodically and unconsciously, the most curious, extravagant and interesting quotations have been extrapolated and collected for future memory. They are phrases which have more than once captured the nature of boxing, the often paradoxical role of the fighter, of his irreverent simplicity, of his fragility in a difficult and often violent discipline.

Our objective is to pay homage to the boxing world; to its anguish, its hope, and its myths in a manner which is both original and disenchanted, searching to maintain that absolute and relative poetic climate that drives us all to admire this sport. It seemed to us that all of this imposed a structure free from constraint and framework. And therefore whoever is looking for a connection between aphorism and photographs will search in vain, and whoever thinks to have found this connection has been too rash and the conclusions drawn will be refuted. Obviously, everything is true until proven otherwise.

Rome, May 1995   The Authors

It might seem to be a paradox, but it is easy to ascertain that the very ancient art of boxing, where it is generally practised and cultivated, becomes a guarantee of peace and meekness. Our nervous aggression, our susceptibility in ambush derive from the depth of our feelings of impotence and physical inferiority. Moreover, we feel disarmed in front of the offence, and the desire torments us to demonstrate to others, and to persuade ourselves, that no one can offend us with impunity. Against this, he who understands the force that his hands possess does not have to persuade anyone about anything.

Maurice Maeterlinck

Tom Sayers knocks out Tom Paddock in the 21st
round, winning the title. Great Britain, June 15,
1858.

*In Germany like in France some of the English terms belonging to the
upper-class sport language were adopted in the eighteenth century. Since
1744 the term "baxen" began to appear in the more cultured form
"boxen".*

Norbert Elias

William Perry (*at left*) strikes Harry Broome's left eye. This technical foul gets him disqualified. Great Britain, September 29, 1851.

The youngest son of Lord Shaftesbury died in 1825 after sixty rounds of a match that lasted two and a half hours against a schoolfellow in Eton, under the other pupils' eyes. His father refused to apply for justice. Notwithstanding the death of his beloved son, it was a fair fight between them.

I'd like more than anything to be the heavyweight champion of the world — which is impossible — than to be the King of England or the President of the United States or the Kaiser of Germany.

Jack London

Opposite page: "Sugar" Ray Leonard rejoices after knocking out Andy Price. Las Vegas, September 28, 1979.
Above: "Sugar" Ray Leonard in a break from his training. October, 1988.

*B*oxing is like abortion, it seems to arouse deep and divisive emotions, though activists who would outlaw abortion are not necessarily those who would outlaw boxing: puritanical instincts take unpredictable forms.

Joyce Carol Oates

The much-anticipated
encounter between Bob
Fitzsimmons and Peter
Maher (*at left*).

*T*he 1986 heavyweight title match between Ruby Robert Fitzsimmons and
*Peter Maher, for instance, was outlawed everywhere in the States, so
promoters staged it on an isolated sandbar in the Rio Grande River, four
hundred miles from El Paso. Three hundred men made the arduous
journey to witness what was surely one of the most disappointing title
bouts in boxing history when Fitzsimmons knocked out Maher in ninety-
five seconds.*

The bigger they are, the harder they fall.

Bob Fitzsimmons

Bob Fitzsimmons.

The longest bare-knuckle fight was in 1855 in Melbourne between fighters Kelly and Smith, it lasted six and one-quarter hours. Even the fights with gloves were, till the 1900s, fought to the bitter end, so much that in 1893 in New Orleans, Andy Bowen and Jack Burke fought 110 rounds for seven hours and nineteen seconds. The match was suspended for darkness and was declared even.

John L. Sullivan, photographed at the end of his career, having fought 35 matches, winning 16 by knockout. The only knockout he suffered, by Jim Corbett, cost him the title.

Primo Carnera with his manager, Luigi Loresi, in 1935.

The most moving moment of boxing history was the immense charitable gesture of Max Schmeling who during the war saved Primo Carnera... this proves that inside that terrifying mental universe brotherhood can miraculously find deep roots.

Alexis Philonenko

Above: Marcel Cerdan wins the world middle-
weight title against Tony Zale by a technical
knockout in the 12th round. Shown here is the final
phase with Zale getting up to the sound of the
bell, but no longer able to fight. Jersey City,
September 21, 1948.
Opposite: Tony Zale.

*Tony Zale had a punch that was like a sword, rapid, violent, elegant. It
was like classic work of literature. It was a Shakespearean punch...*
Walter Chiari

Tony Zale

Enzo Fiermonte. *Above:* With his wife Madeline Force Astor.

There have been unforgettable figures. Primo Carnera, who after everything that happened to him could have inspired a novel the level of Gone With the Wind, *or Fiermonte, who wasn't phenomenal in the ring, but with his escape to the court of an American millionaire could have inspired miles of film. Also Bosisio and Mitri; all really special people in the sport and in their lives. If fact, there is no shortage of role models for literature and Italian cinema to study boxing.*

Roberto Fazi

Above: Joe Louis strikes Billy Conn.
New York, June 18, 1941.
Opposite: Joe Louis with a fan.

Some time ago one of the southern states adopted a new method of capital punishment. Poison gas supplanted the gallows. In its earliest stages, a microphone was placed inside the sealed death chamber so that scientific observers might hear the words of the dying prisoner. The first victim was a young Negro. When the cyanide tablet was dropped into the container and the gas curled upwards, through the microphone came these words: "Save me, Joe Louis, save me, Joe Lewis, save me, Joe Lewis."

Martin Luther King

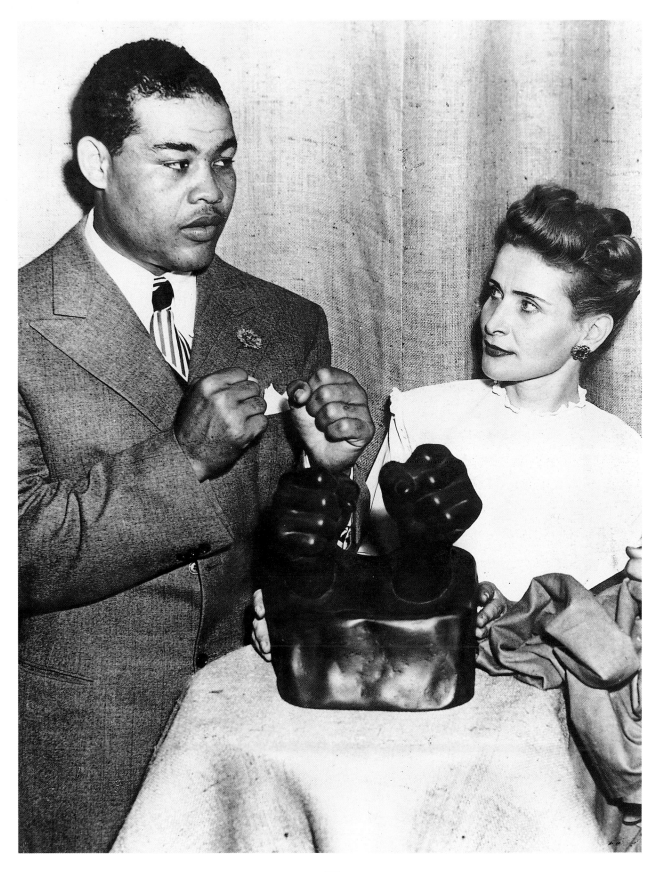

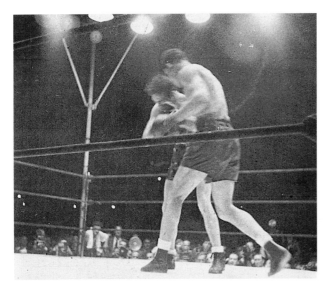

He can run [Billy Conn] but he can't hide.

Joe Louis

Joe Louis beats Billy Conn. The dramatic sequences
of theknockout in the 13th round.
New York, June 18, 1941.

Opposite, above: Tiberio Mitri and Jake La Motta.
New York, July 12, 1950.

I don't care if I die in the ring.

Jake La Motta

My family was so poor that every Christmas Eve my father would go outside the house and fire some gun shots. Then he'd come back in and tell us that Santa Claus killed himself.

Jake La Motta

All sports are intrinsically competitive and so they tend to encourage aggressiveness and violence to rise. But in some of them, for example rugby, soccer and boxing, the violence is the central ingredient in the form of a "fun fight" or "mock battle" between two individuals or groups. Such sports are the socially acceptable and ritualised expression of physical violence.

Eric Dunning

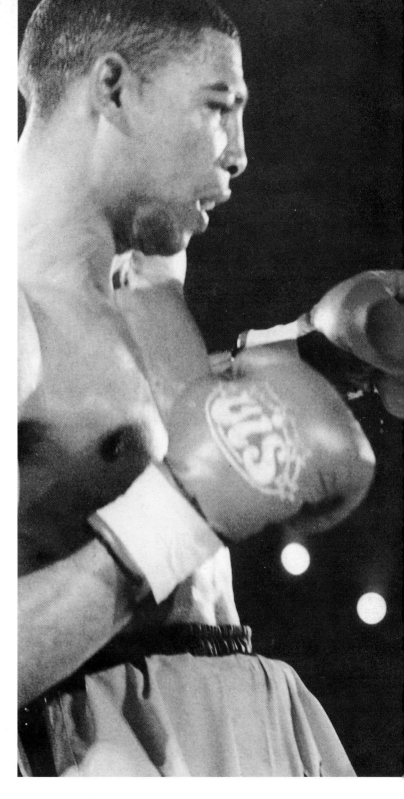

Giovanni Parisi
and Michael Ayers.
Rome, April 16, 1993.

I ain't never loved violence.

"Sugar" Ray Robinson

In the corner they told me that it wasn't the end of the second round but the end of the sixth round. It's all black, there is a mystery of fifteen minutes in my brain. What happened from the third to the sixth round? It is a vacuum, a complete vacuum.

Aldo Spoldi

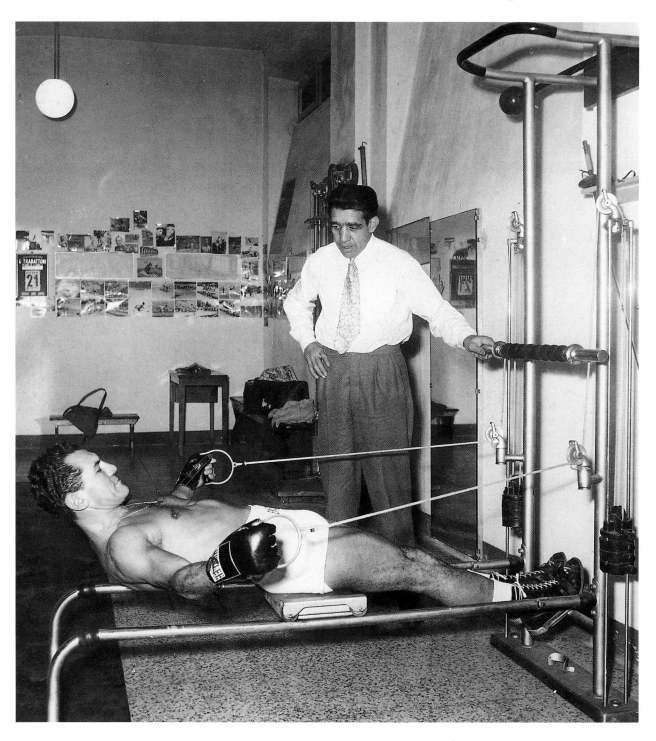

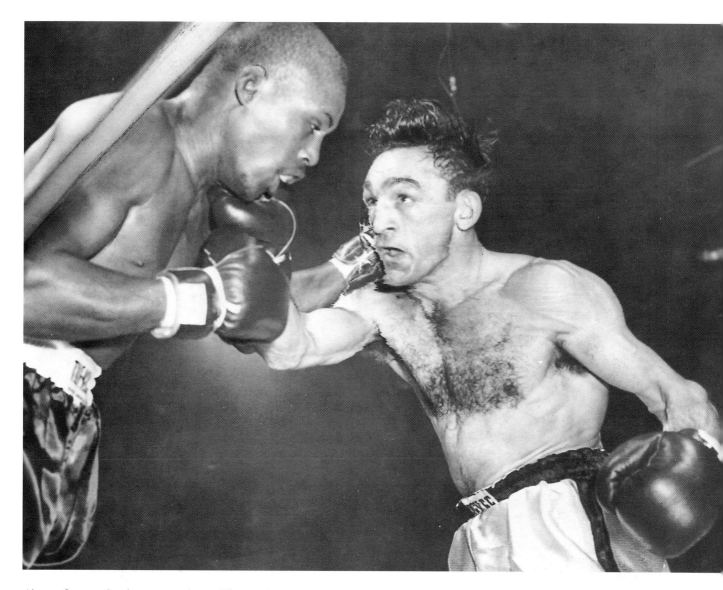

Above: Carmen Basilio regains the middle-weight
title against Johnny Saxton. Syracuse, September
12, 1956.
Opposite: Aldo Spoldi trains in the gym of
Amedeo Dejana in 1952.

I can't concentrate when I play golf or go bowling: I could only do it in
the ring. Bowling balls are not going to hit me.

Carmen Basilio

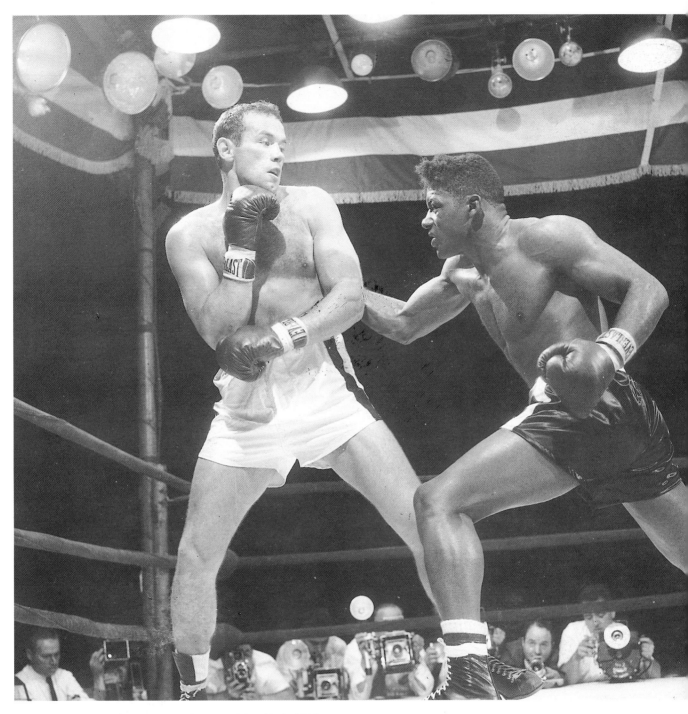

Floyd Patterson attacks Ingemar Johansson, New York, 1960.

If a fighter has a match in him, you can be sure he's saving it for me.
Floyd Patterson

I've never been knocked out.
I've been unconsciousness, but
it's always been on my feet.
Floyd Patterson

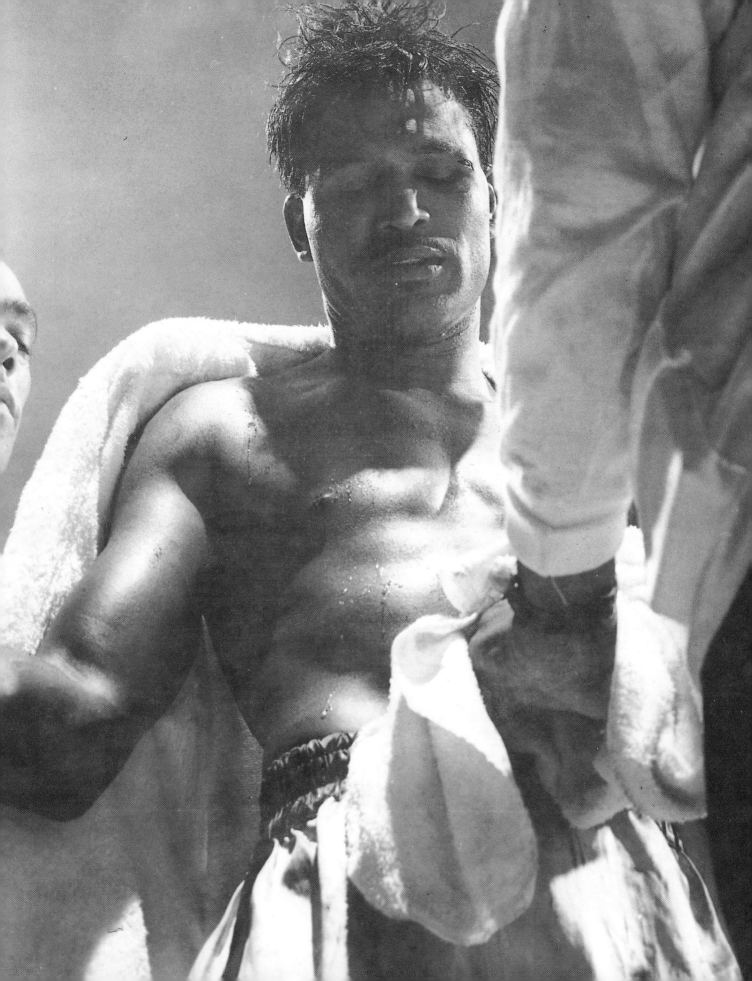

Opposite: "Sugar" Ray Robinson leaves the ring after his defeat by Gene Fullmer. New York, January 2, 1957.
Above: A phase of the match between the challenger Archie Moore and Rocky Marciano. New York, September 21, 1955.

I've met "Sugar" Ray so many times that it's a miracle I haven't become diabetic.

Jake La Motta

Teofilo Stevenson is proclaimed the winner. Reno, November 13, 1986.

I never cared very much about physical means. I think that in the ring, the most important thing is intelligence.

Teofilo Stevenson

Patterson slips on the mat in the match against Archie Moore. Chicago, November 30, 1956.

*W*hen Liston knocked Patterson out he stayed on the mat. He was lucky. When Liston knocked me out, I went up like an idiot and he knocked me out again.

Tullus Mead

Opposite: Primo Carnera in training in 1934.
Above: Carnera exhibits himself in the gym.
New York, 1949.

*N*othing can give you as much satisfaction as success in the ring. It's so wonderful that even if you lose and they hurt you can't wait to have another occasion to try again.

Primo Carnera

Rocky Marciano. *Opposite:* His right strikes Joe
Louis. New York, October 26, 1951.

*Rocky Marciano trained with the most monastic devotion; his training
methods have become legendary. Marciano concentrated on one thing: the
upcoming fight. Every minute of his life was defined in terms of the
opening second of the fight. In his training camp the opponent's name
was never mentioned in Marciano's hearing... Marciano would not write
a letter; take telephone calls, nor meet new acquaintances during the last
ten days before a fight. During the week before the fight he would not
shake hands. Or go for a ride in a car, or eat new foods! All of his
attention, his intelligence, all of his passion and his emotion were
directed toward the opponent he would fight.*

Joyce Carol Oates

Joe Frazier. London, June 26, 1973.

Muhammad Ali raises "Sugar" Ray Robinson's arm. Drew Bundini cries.

He [Muhammad Ali] kept on telling me, "You can't hit me, you can't hit me — I'm God". At the end I couldn't take it anymore and I told him, "You might be God, but today I'll beat you".

Joe Frazier

Teofilo Stevenson strikes Biagio Chianese. Los
Angeles, April 14, 1984.

You always have to have respect for the one in front of you.
Teofilo Stevenson

*N*ever *during the time I have spent boxing have I been interested in
becoming professional.*

Teofilo Stevenson

*W*hen *I was younger I thought I was like Floyd Patterson, then I
realised that I'm only like myself.*

Teofilo Stevenson

Floyd Patterson retains his world title by beating
Tommy Jackson by a technical knockout in the 10th
round. On the left is the speaker Harry Balogh, on
the right trainer Nick Florio. New York, July 29, 1957.

Mike Tyson's straight right falls on Trevor Berbick. Las Vegas, November 22, 1986.

In the ring I knew I was different. I could let the violence out that I felt exploding in me, and at the same time stay within the rules that as a man I reject.

Mike Tyson

Joe Frazier.

I *don't want to knock out my opponent. I want to hit him, step away,*
and watch him hurt. I want his heart.

Joe Frazier

Above: Larry Holmes and his trainer Eddie Futch. June, 1982.
Opposite: Referee Mills Lane raises the arm of
Larry Holmes at the end of the match against
Gerry Cooney. Las Vegas, June 11, 1982.

*It's hard being black. Ever been black? I was black once — when I was
poor.*

Larry Holmes

Opposite: Gene Tunney prepares himself for his
match against Tom Heeney, his final match. July, 1928.
Above: Gene Tunney in 1937.

*Greb gave me a terrible whipping, he broke my nose, maybe with a
butt. He cut my eyes and ears. My jaw was swollen from the right temple
down the cheek, along under the chin and partway up the other side. But
it was in that first fight, in which I lost my American light-heavyweight
title, that I knew I had found a way to beat Harry Greb eventually. I
was fortunate, really. If boxing in those days had been afflicted with the
Commission doctors we have today — The first fight with Greb would
have been stopped before I learned how to beat him. It's possible, even
probable, that if this had happened I would never have been heard of
again.*

Gene Tunney

Rocky's restaurant, Miami, Florida.

*W*hen it's all over, I'm going to write a book on my life. Here's the title: The Only Square Thing Was the Ring.

Bob Biron

Musing upon the age difference between Larry Holmes and Mike Tyson in the challenge for the world title. London, January, 1988.

*J*ust between us, I prefer boxers to intellectuals.

Alexis Philonenko

Marcel Cerdan strikes Tony Zale with a straight punch.
Jersey City, September 21, 1948.

In boxing the primordial instinct of man lives. The same instinct that this society tries to repress, to destroy. Boxing lets me express myself, my anger, my hate. They were sentiments born from frustrated desires, in front of the emptiness of society. I've never been able to free myself from that fury, nor will I ever. I can only live with it

Mickey Rourke

I hate to say it, but it's true — I only like it better when pain comes.
Frank "The Animal" Fletcher

Frank Fletcher is sent to the mat by a punch from Juan Roldan.
Las Vegas, November 10, 1983.

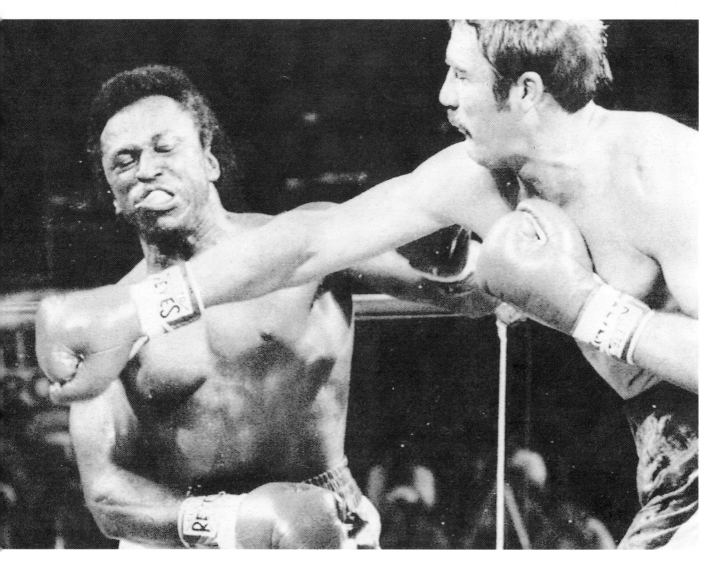

Gerrie Coetzee strikes Michael Dokes.
Richfield, September 24, 1983.

I am not interested in discussions about races. I can't see any colour but the red of the gloves and the red of blood. I don't care about black or white but a left or right.

Gerrie Coetzee

Marcel Cerdan being embraced by his brother and Georges Carpentier (at left).
Jersey City, September 21, 1948.

*E*ach boxing match is a story — A unique and highly condensed drama
without words. Even when nothing sensational happens: then the drama
is "merely" psychological. Therefore it is extraordinary.

Joyce Carol Oates

José Torres.

I would fight anybody. I didn't care who they were. I even wanted to fight Joe Louis. But that made me win. They would hit me. I didn't care if I got hit.

Jake La Motta

We fighters understand lies. What's a feint? What's a left hook off the jab? What's an opening? What's thinking one thing and doing another?

José Torres

Jake La Motta after the match with Tiberio Mitri.
New York, July 21, 1950.

You got to get the hard-on, and then you got to keep it. You want to be careful not to lose the hard-on, and cautious not to come.

Drew "Bundini" Brown
to Cassius Clay

Muhammad Ali, in his training camp in N'Sele, psychologically prepares for the fight with Foreman with "war" cries to the sound of drums. Behind him are his trainer Drew Bundini and aide Gene Kilroy. Zaire, October 1974.

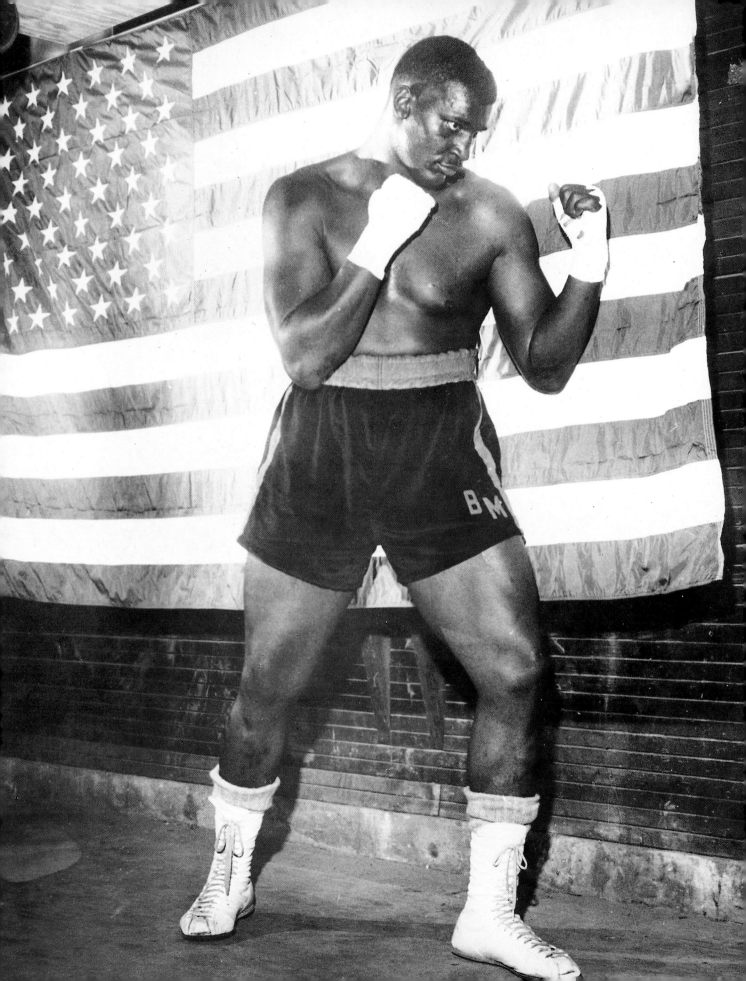

Above, opposite: Buster Mathis.

*T*he only thing I know about managers is that when the bell sounds, I
go one way into the middle of the ring and they go the other way out of
it.

Buster Mathis

*B*oxing is the sport to which all other sports aspire.

George Foreman

Do you like jazz? It is like boxing. The more beautiful, the fewer people appreciate it.

George Foreman

Above: George Foreman faces Michael Moorer.
Las Vegas, November 5, 1994.
Opposite: George Foreman the day after his
victory over Terry Anderson. London, September 26, 1990.

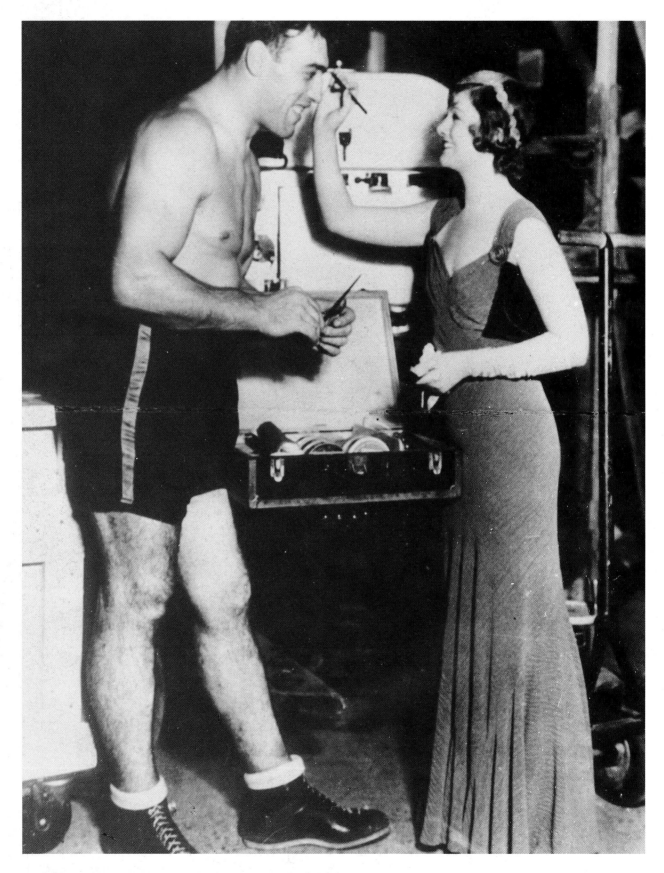

Primo Carnera was 2.07 meters tall.
Opposite: With Mirna Loy.

*D*uring the 1920s when boxing was officially banned in New York, boxers fought without any medical control. Clandestinely. Every neighbourhood had a club where they fought illegally every night. There were more matches then than there are today.

Budd Schulberg

Willie Pep defeats Ray Famechon. New York, March 17, 1950.

*The decline of a boxer. First you lose your leg movement. Then you lose
your reflexes. Then you lose your friends.*

Willie Pep

Willie Pep prepares himself for his 2nd victory over Sandy Saddler. Middletown, September, 1951.

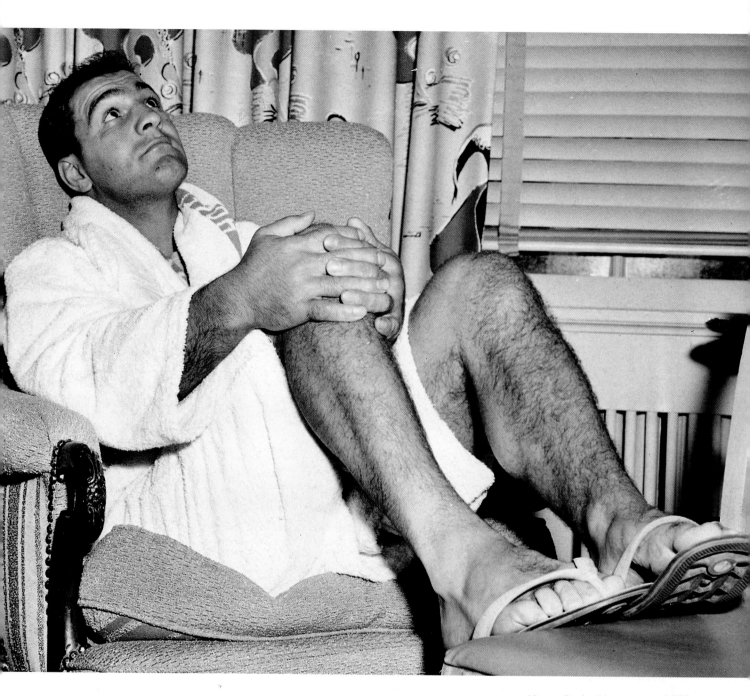

Above: Rocky Marciano in 1955.
Opposite: Primo Carnera in 1934.

*D*empsey was alone and Tunney could never explain himself and
Sharkey could never believe himself. Carnera was sad. Bear an
indecipherable clown. The great heavy-weight fighters like Louis had the
lonliness of the ages in their silence...

Norman Mailer

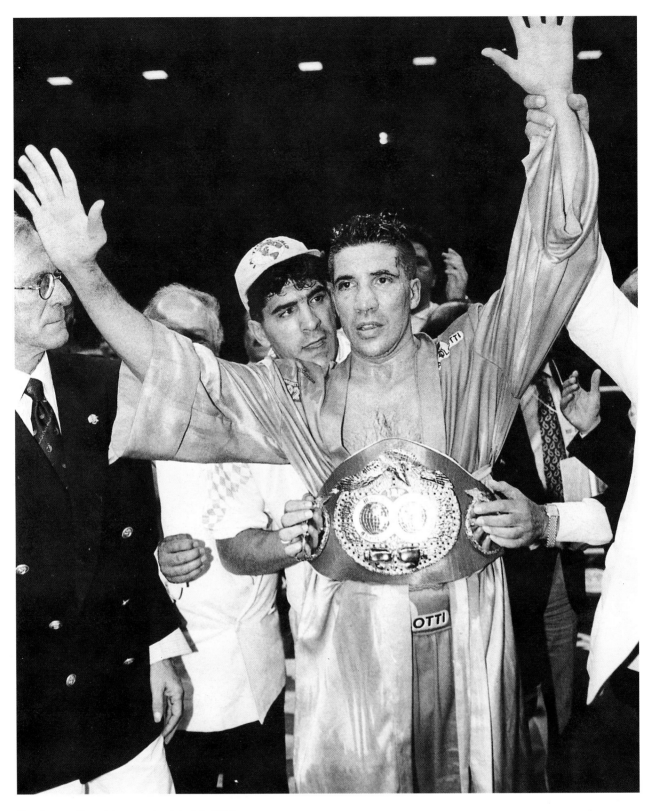

Gianfranco Rosi. Montecarlo, July 11, 1992.

Boy, a champion like that wouldn't even consider you worthy of a glance! Go and make a reputation, he would say!".
"I can hit him whenever I want", answered the boy.
"Yes of course, but the public doesn't know it. If you hit him like you say, you would become the world champion! And nobody can do it the first match...".
"Well, I can".

Jack London

Ray Leonard interviews Marvin Hagler after the match against Fulgencio Obelmejias.
Sanremo, Italy, October 31, 1982.

Tommy Hearns was a little cocky, and I had something for him.

Marvin Hagler

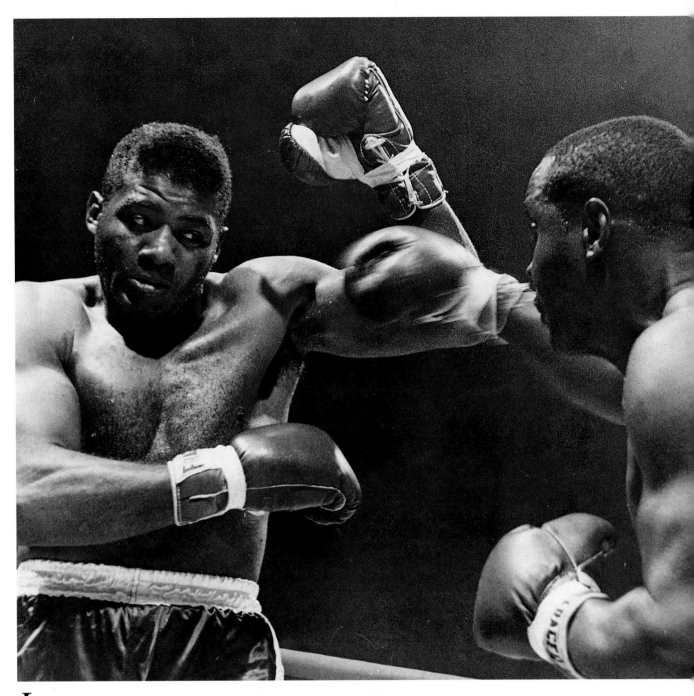

Liston was a colossus with hands bigger than hams, so much that he couldn't find a glove size that would fit him.

Nat Fleischer

When I was a boy the only things that could really hurt me were my father's eyes. Everytime I came home late and found him drunk, I was afraid of his stares which hurt me more than his belts.

Sonny Liston

Sonny Liston strikes Floyd Patterson. Las Vegas, July 22, 1963.

Liston had a sinister face and behind him a questionable past. In the United States it was inconceivable that an ex-convict could become champion of the world. But in the end everyone had to face the real valor that he possessed. He was as strong as Louis and his hook was terrifying.
Roberto Fazi

Charles "Sonny" Liston.

*W*hen a boxer is "knocked out" it does not mean, as it's commonly thought, that he has been knocked unconscious, or even incapacitated; it means rather more poetically that he has been knocked out of Time.

Joyce Carol Oates

Opposite: Nino Benvenuti watches the counting of Sandro Mazzinghi. Milan, Italy, June 18, 1965.
Above: With Carlos Monzon.

I wanted to tackle Monzon. I had to take on that risk. I could have put off that match. But I was the champion and I had to take the risk on. I couldn't swerve from the reality. Because only if you go with your head held high are you a real champion.

Nino Benvenuti

*If I didn't have a knock-out
punch it was because I
interpreted with style the
harmony of the movement,
what is syncrony, what is
beauty. An art. A Noble Art.
Punches? Padded punches.
Violence? A vibrant force,
art.*
                Tiberio Mitri

Tiberio Mitri.

*I was improved with boxing.
I became punctilious and
disciplined. I liked talking to
cultured people because I
learned something. The
Noble Art opened up for me
the world that I dreamed
about when I was a boy.*
                Tiberio Mitri

Ray Robinson dodges Rocky Graziano's left.
Chicago, April 16, 1952.

It's a terrible sport but it's a sport. The fight in the ring is the struggle for survival.

Rocky Graziano

In American boxing, I have always liked Stanley Ketchel, the world middle-weight champion during the beginning of the 1900s. He was a type who could challenge Jack Johnson, who weighed 20 kilos more than him, and put him on the carpet with ferocious cunning, even if he paid a high price; when Jack got back up he sent Ketchel to the carpet knocking out his teeth. Ketchel was a great character — He was handsome, tall and blond. He was shot to death at the age of 24 by a jealous husband in San Francisco. Paul Newman could have played him splendidly, like he did Rocky Graziano in Someone Up There Likes Me.

Roberto Fazi

Robinson and Graziano joke around during the medical visit.
Chicago, April 16, 1952.

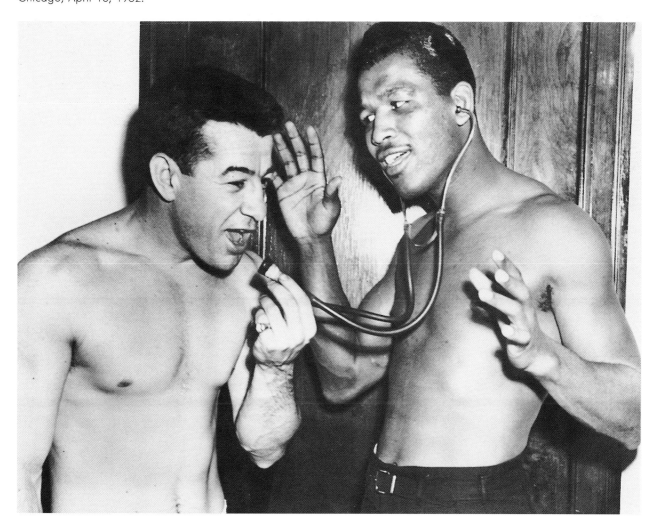

I love boxing because it has the foundations of science, the magic of geometry: the long stroke, the short one, the range of action, angles and swerves. It is like a mind applied to science. Like the human figure of Leonardo da Vinci.

Walter Chiari

Floyd Patterson's right falls on Tommy "Hurricane" Jackson.
New York, July 29, 1957.

I'm not a delinquent. I've never killed anyone, never mortally wounded anybody. I'm just a child of the New York ghetto. Anyone who's been there knows what that means.

Mike Tyson

Opposite: Mike Tyson after his victory over James Smith.
Las Vegas, March 7, 1987.
Above: Tyson receives an honory doctorate in
Literature from Central State University,
Wilberforce, Ohio April 26, 1989.

I don't have any friends. I get paranoid around people. I can only relax in the locker room before the fight. That is the best time... I don't care very much about my opponents then.

Mike Tyson

It is legitimate to ask if the match does not irresistably lead to the moment when the two men embrace, men who otherwise both in public and in private, could never approach one another with such passion.

Joyce Carol Oates

Opposite: Eddie Perkins with Duilio Loi.
Above: Perkins in Milan, Italy, September 4, 1962.

If they cut my bald head open, they will find one big boxing glove. That's all I am. I live it.

Marvin Hagler

*Y*ou have to take care of them during training, during the matches and after the matches; you have to teach them the federal regulations, to have respect for the referee and judges, to accept verdicts whatever they are without protesting or complaining, to respect adversaries and others, with modesty and friendship.

Steve Klaus

Above: Three world champions — Jersey Joe Walcott, Ezzard Charles, and Rocky Marciano — joke with the young Billy Ryan. Boston, May 29, 1957.
Opposite: Steve Klaus and Duilio Loi.

A boxer (in the third round) to the corner: "How am I doing?"
The manager (looking at the opponent): "If you kill him you're even."

Beppe Viola

Above, opposite: Giovanni Parisi.

In the ring, one and against the other, everything cancels out. Everything starts from the beginning. And then once again.

Giovanni Parisi

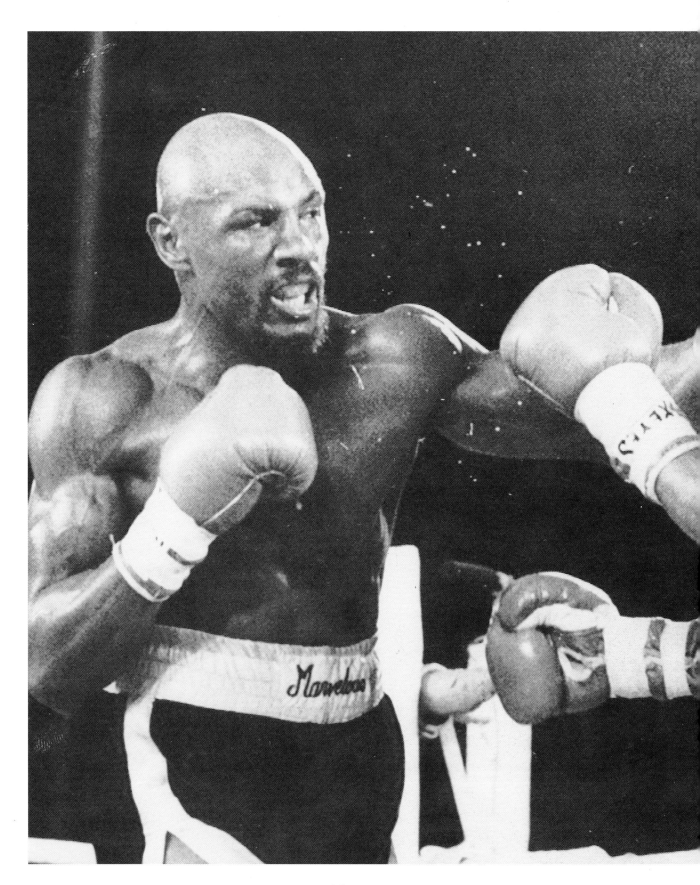

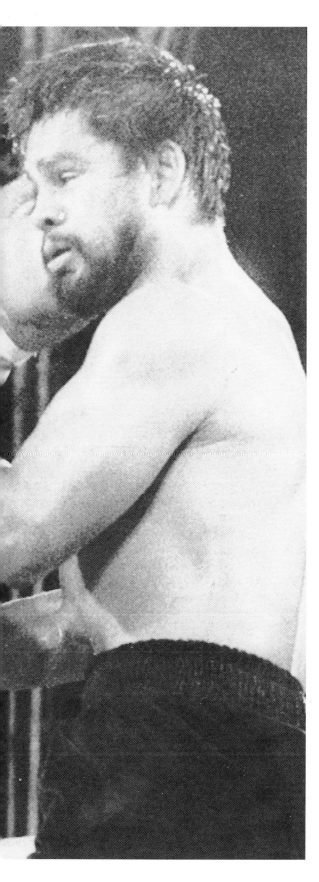

*I am a fighter who walks, talks, and thinks
fighting, but I try not to look like it.*

Marvin Hagler

Marvin Hagler strikes the challenger Roberto
Duran. Las Vegas, November 10, 1983.

I knew how hard my strokes were, and I tried to check them when I could. It was a good thing. My awareness helped me respect my opponent's blows that eventually had the honour to knock me out.

Federico Friso

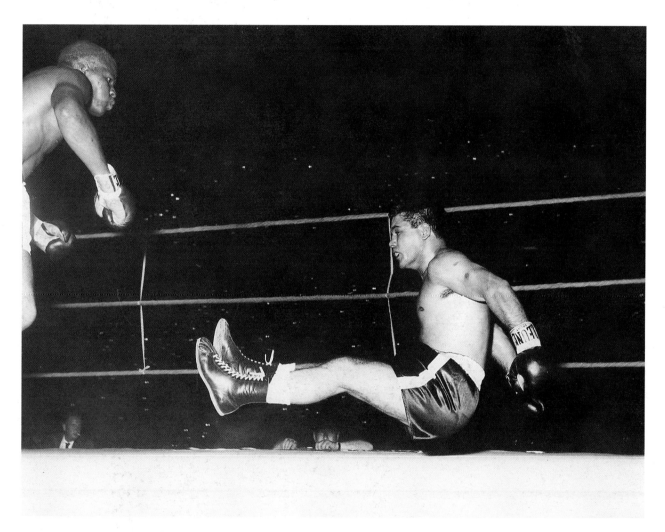

Above: Italo Scortichini is sent to the mat by a punch from Eddie Thompson. Milan, Italy, September, 1960.
Opposite: Federico Friso.

Boxing taught me to react to blows below the belt, to misfortune, to disgrace, to injustice, and the things you can avoid because in the ring you have to take the hits. It taught me to suffer, squandering all your energies — and to win.

Walter Chiari

Above: Sonny Liston dances the twist with his wife Geraldine.
Opposite: "Sugar" Ray Robinson. London, September 4, 1962.

"*B*oxing can give me incredible human moments and psychological fragments. About a boxer's suffering, about the pathos surrounding him, about his reacting capabilities, about a more general human metaphor. And then I like the boxing spectator. His capacity to identify with the favourite at all costs, like the other one was not a simple adversary but an absolute enemy to defeat by all means.

Morando Morandini

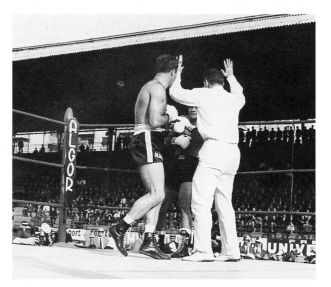

I don't consider boxing a metaphor for something else. I can only take into consideration that life is a metaphor for boxing — for one of those bouts that go on and on, round following round, jabs, failed punches, clinches, nothing determined, again the bell and again and you and your opponent so evenly matched it's impossible not to see that your opponent is you.

Joyce Carol Oates

*T*here wasn't anyone to tie me to amateurism. On the contrary, I received a lot of offers to become professional, but I wanted to go to the Olympic Games. I have to say that from the first time I stepped into the gym, my goal was to go to the Olympics.

Nino Benvenuti

*Am I afraid of the ring? Heck, I worked in a chemical company and
had to clean the floors with reagent chemicals. Breathing those
chemicals, I could have died faster there than in the ring.*

Michael Spinks

He [Muhammad Ali] worked apparently on the premise that here was something obscene about being hit.

Norman Mailer

Muhammad Ali's straight right
strikes Doug Jones.
New York, March 13, 1963.

Rocky Marciano.

Floyd Patterson.

The mind of a heavyweight champion is full of thoughts without answers, of thoughts that strike terror into their hearts.

Norman Mailer

Primo Carnera.

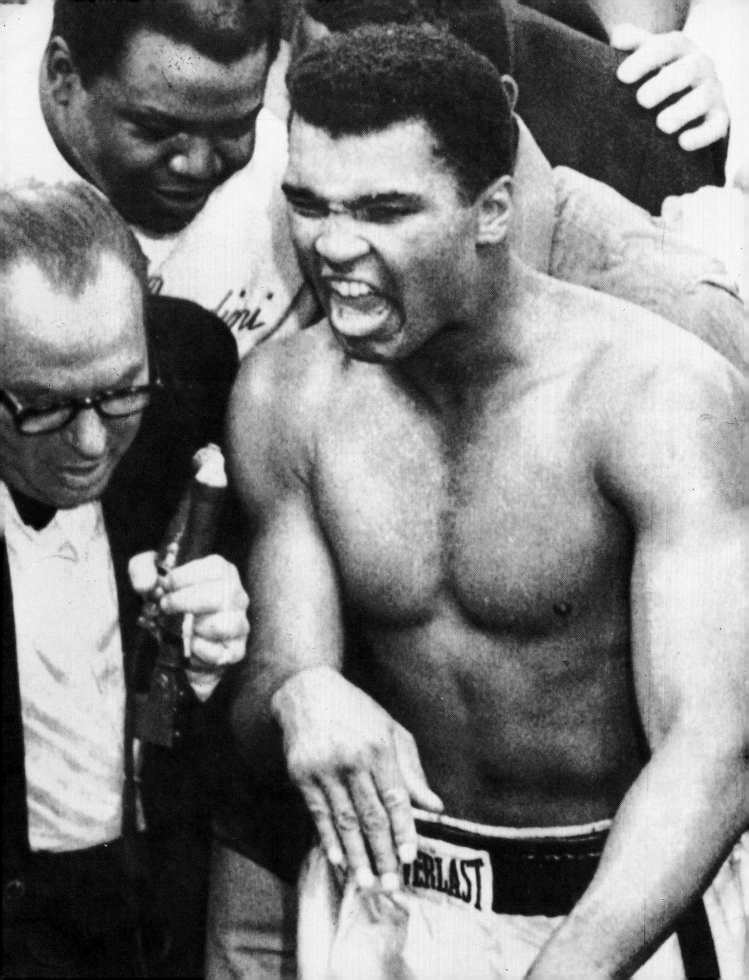

*D*uring matches when I made fun of my opponents, my aggressiveness followed a plan, the same as it happens in many human activities.

Muhammad Ali

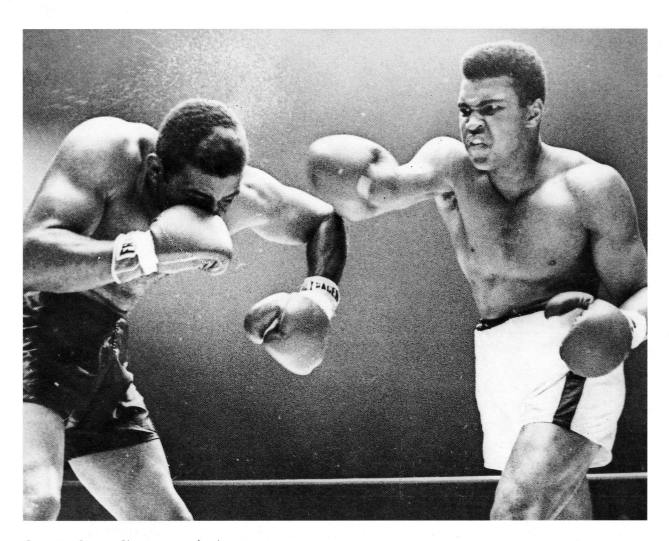

Opposite: Cassius Clay rejoices after his victory over Sonny Liston. Lewiston, Maine, May 25, 1965.
Above: Cassius Clay strikes Floyd Patterson.
Las Vegas, November 22, 1965.

*W*hen you're as great as I am, it's difficult to be modest.

Muhammad Ali

*B*oxing is a trade, but not for those who practice it.

Roland Passevent

Above: Cassius Clay and Lionel Hampton predict
the defeat of Sonny Liston in the 8th round.
New York, 1963.
Opposite: "Sugar" Ray Robinson. Hollywood,
October, 1969.

A lot of people have told me that when I play the trumpet I look like a
boxer. Probably it's true. I think I am an aggressive person especially for
things I believe in, like when I have to play. So I fight till the last drop
of sweat.

Miles Davis

*E*very talent must unfold itself in the fighting.

Friedrich Nietzsche

I am the greatest.

Muhammad Ali

Below: Cassius Clay celebrates his birthday
thinking about Sonny Liston. Miami, January 17, 1964.
Opposite: Cassius Clay's victory over Sonny Liston.

Patrizio Oliva in the match against the Frenchman
Charles Jurietti. Formia, Italy, July 7, 1981.

I didn't want to meet Coggi. He was an unknown. I didn't care anything about him. I wanted to end my career in glory. They proposed Camacho but nothing came of it. Meanwhile I continued my training. This is how Coggi the unknown got there. I went in the ring empty. For the first time I had underestimated an adversary. The ring never forgave me.

Patrizio Oliva

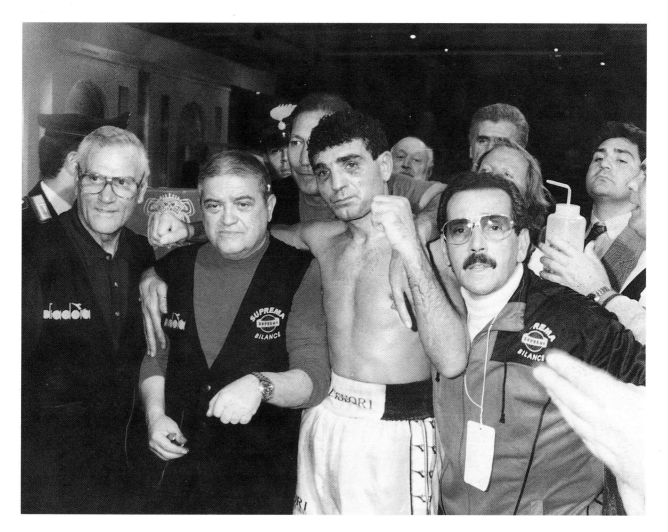

Patrizio Olivia embraces Rocco Agostino after the match.

Jack Dempsey

When you're fighting, you're fighting for one thing: money.

Jack Dempsey

Jack Dempsey forces Tommy Gibbons to surrender.
Montana, July 4, 1923.

You always think you're going to win the match, that you'll dominate your opponent, otherwise you couldn't fight at all.

Jack Dempsey

Cassius Clay in training. 1963

I was so fast that I could get up, cross the room, turn off the light and get back in bed before the light went off.

Muhammad Ali

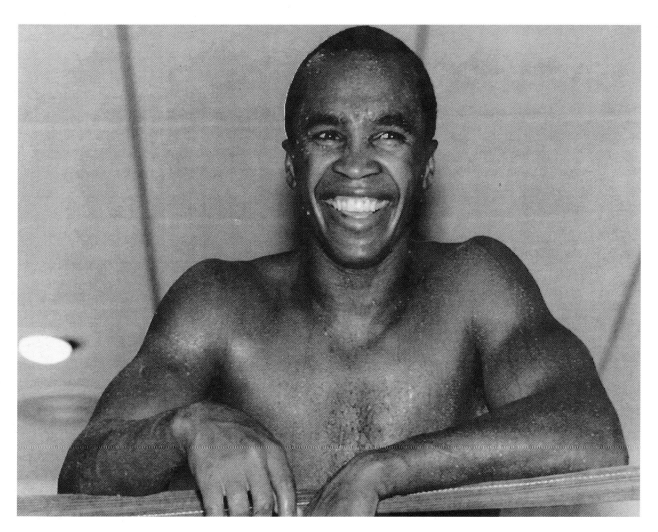

"Sugar" Ray Leonard in 1988.

I box, but not a lot because it seems a little absurd for a president to appear in public with a black eye or a smashed nose or with cut lips.

Theodore Roosevelt

"It's enough just to beat the other guys", I yelled during the weigh-in, "but you [Tyrell Biggs] I really want to hurt." He held out seven rounds. That was good, I couldn't have thrown on him all the punches I wanted in only one round.

Mike Tyson

Above: Mike Tyson at his weigh-in for the match
against Trevor Berbick. Las Vegas, November 21, 1986.
Opposite: Mike Tyson in 1988.

In the ring I feel like I can't be betrayed, except by myself. The ring is the most beautiful place in the world. You know what can happen.

Mike Tyson

*T*hough male spectators identify with boxers no boxer behaves like a "normal" man when he is in the ring and no combination of blows is "natural". All is style.

Joyce Carol Oates

"Sugar" Ray Robinson in training.

Of all the sports, the only one that I really love is boxing. Of course, little by little it is a sport which is disappearing. I hope that in the remaining days that I have in this life that there will always be an arena somewhere where I can go.

Jack London

Index of Boxers

125

Index of Quotations